MAJESTIC CUT

Emily Carlson

Fernwood
PRESS

Majestic Cut

Fernwood Press
Newberg, Oregon
www.fernwoodpress.com

Printed in the United States of America

Page design: Mareesa Fawver Moss
Cover image: Jules Carlson
Author photo: Meg Shevenock

ISBN 978-1-59498-228-6

For my brilliant and beloved mother

Contents

COMPLETION THROUGH REMOVAL
COMPLETION THROUGH COLLAPSE
COMPLETION THROUGH EMPTINESS

—Gordon Matta-Clarke, written on a notecard

PREFACE

I have made majestic cuts while writing this book. I have changed some names, made real people composite characters, transposed events, imagined dialogue. It happened but not in this way. Not like I say it did.

As Thich Nhất Hạnh writes, "An electron is first of all your concept of the electron." How can we see a person beyond our perception of them, beyond the limits and limitations of our own mind? What does it take for a person to become real to us? For us to become real to ourselves?

A story. A gust of wind lifting the branches. I shaped it into something that I can hold. The truest story isn't always told according to the facts. The heart feels beyond.

PROOF

Our first time alone together for almost ten years, my mother and I stay in a hotel at the edge of an old-growth forest. After dusk, we follow a path into a grove, tips of white pines vanishing in the moonless dark. A friend has told her, "If you photograph the trees at night, you'll see orbs."

The narrative I've made for my mother is that, before leaving her husband, she wants proof she isn't alone in the cosmos.

An internet search for "orbs" yields another term: backscatter, an optical phenomenon resulting in often circular artifacts on an image, attributed to the camera's flash being reflected from unfocused motes of dust, water droplets, or other particles in the air or water.

As soon as I tell "what happened" there's this nagging feeling that the story I'm telling isn't true. The experience falls away, the world falls away, and all I can do is hold the essence in my hands.

In essence, what the cutting does is to make the [memory] more articulated and to produce unexpected views and an aspect of stratification: the thin edge, the severed surface reveals the autobiographical process of its making, overlapping readings of conditions past and present.

I held my mother's stories as if they were her. As, for example, the time when—

Mom leans over the page and whispers: "Don't tell the neck part. It's not even accurate. Charlie didn't put his hands around my neck when I was in the shower, he—"

"Maybe you could say instead, 'He put his shoe in her mouth.' Or, 'One afternoon, standing in their backyard, the great drifts of white cloud looked to her like a woman being choked by a monster.'"

ENOUGH

Before they were married, Charlie came to our apartment for dinner. "I'll save you from the leftovers," he said and served himself a second helping.

In an earlier draft of this book, I wrote: That night, tucking the sheet under my chin, my mother whispered, "That was all our food for the week."

MOM: I didn't tell you that. I would never have put a child in the middle.

How did I know it was all our food for the week? The look on her face? A sensation in my body? Did I hear her thinking it? The truth is, I felt her feeling it. Or, perhaps, I felt a feeling I thought was her feeling it.

MOM: Maybe you overheard me talking to my sister on the phone.

Poor Mom, I thought, *she's worried about feeding her child.*

MOM: We were so broke. Rusty sat me up on a bar stool at the Harmony Inn and said, "A dollar a kiss."

It appeared we couldn't all win at once.

A plan for each bite. To have more than enough, enough, not enough.

In Mom's closet, beneath a sweater I loved to put my face in and smell, she kept an antique bowl, hand painted with roses and dogwood blossoms, that she added spare change to for special occasions.

Why didn't Mom ask Dad for more child support? Why didn't she tell Charlie we needed that food?

My friend sent me Wallace Stevens's "The Auroras of Autumn." *Farewell to an idea ... The mother's face, / The purpose of the poem, fills the room. / [...] The house is evening, half dissolved. / Only the half they can never possess remains, / Still-starred.*

Beneath the poem my friend wrote, "People love to blame the mother, and I don't think it's always fair."

BRONCO

I loved Charlie's truck. That we could ride without seatbelts on the bench seat. The spare tire with a picture of a bucking bronco. Mom wore a ring again. I kept putting baby's breath in his hair. It was thick, brown like my father's, wilder with the windows down, air coming in so fast I couldn't breathe.

Broncos tend to buck when they're frightened or anticipate pain.

It happened all the time / It didn't happen at all.

With my sister's birth came new words: rising chest, cradle cap, startle, root. Palmar grasp: how she clenched my finger. Soft spot: where her skull would fuse. Though I couldn't make the fighting stop, I could touch her soft spot. I could feel it begin to close. I could sigh with relief.

Charlie stood square and taught me how to punch. *Throw, throw, throw*, into his bicep, hard as a barbell. He threw one at me, in jest, leaving a bruise I liked on my body. But "Oww," I said and rubbed it. "Stop," Mom said from their bed beyond the closed door. "We're just having fun," he insisted. We were. I was. But my mother couldn't like what he was teaching me.

"Don't write that. That's my story. That's my life. That's between him and me," Mom wrote in the margin.

How can one separate birdsong from the forest, the life of a child from the life of the mother?

"You're right," Mom said. "But you didn't live it in my body."

Didn't I?

At one, two, three years old, we don't perceive a separate self.

"Our separation of each other is an optical illusion of consciousness," said Einstein.

Unlike figures in coloring books, I saw no bold line around my body. No border to remind me where I began, that I didn't have to let others' emotions swirl through me like great drifts of white cloud.

Guitars hung from their necks in the hallway.

I had to crane my neck to see inside.

Comfort was putting my face in a horse's neck.

He put his hands around hers.

The metal trinket on her necklace spun.

The fact of feeling others' feelings.

"Feelings aren't facts," says a friend in AA. Fact in memoir is a slippery slope.

At Hotlicks, Charlie kissed Mom at the bar, his hand on her jeans while I bounced my baby sister. When dinner came, he talked to me the whole time. My favorite story was about him eating a dozen rose heads on a dare. Other stories I begged for: cop chases, astral travel, jumping trains, how his left ear came half-off. "See this," he said and pulled the lobe so I could touch the hidden scar.

MOM: When I showed a few pages of your book to Rusty, he said, "The mother is not you."

And he said, "Artists use poetic license. We all have the ability to distort what happened, altering words and adding white space. Remember in design school when you drew a room without a ceiling?"

EATING TRASH

"Hildy!" Mom called, and her dog came bounding.

When Hildy scrounged for scraps in the garbage, we would scold in a deepening voice. "Shame, shame." Head on the floor, Hildy would whimper, covering her eyes with her paws.

MOM: Emily, Hildy never ate from the trash, she was the easiest dog.

How does Hildy feel eating from the trash when she never ate from the trash? How do the other dogs feel going unmentioned, unnamed? Why are there sinkholes in memory? How does Hildy feel not eating from the trash when she loved to eat from the trash?

Some [memories] are a tremendous void with very little surface.

My sister and I were always hanging out the windows of the house.

I remember Mom telling me, "He threw the dog off the back porch." I remember holding Hildy, stroking her fur, eyeing the eight-foot drop.

MOM: He did throw her. But I never would have told you that.

Mom washed our clothes and hung them out to dry. The line sagged with their weight. Washed and dried so many times the shirts became translucent. As I walked toward them, I couldn't see the shirts at all. As if they hadn't existed in the first place.

The sweaters, too, had changed. Shrunken beyond recognition, when my sister and I tried them on, they didn't fit.

Had I grabbed someone else's load and mistaken it for ours?

The mind holds the *I* like a shield as if to say, *Here is something.*

What if it isn't?

Stage left. My first stepfather was beloved to me. Caught me in his arms. Wrote epic notes in looping script and tucked them in my lunch box. Spun me until I couldn't walk straight. Made up songs for me on his guitar. Leapt over me on park benches. Roller-skated backward while singing, the baby in his arms. Taught me to run without making a sound.

Became translucent. Didn't fit. Enter stage right. Another man. Another marriage. Or perhaps he entered in the foreground in half-hidden masses of land. In the story I'm telling I call them the same made-up name. Their shirts in the washer all tangled in a knot.

The knot of marriage? When the ends are pulled, it becomes so strong that the rope will break before the knot comes undone is an image that terrifies me. I wanted my mother to leave him.

Me? I played the same role.

Evenings before my sister and I went to bed, I placed my hands on the piano keys. If I play Brahms' "Lullaby" perfectly, the fighting will stop. I didn't focus on the notes, I focused on perfection. How many times did I start over?

That the mind can smooth a jagged intake of breath. Change the knot in the washer, the shirts on the line. Bend the grass where horses graze. Admit light where there was none.

Where is "thingness" to be found?

The sun passed across the back porch. At first the cut [in the memory] had a very different shape. I studied it over the course of a year and changed the shape until it defined an arc. The arc followed the beam of light.

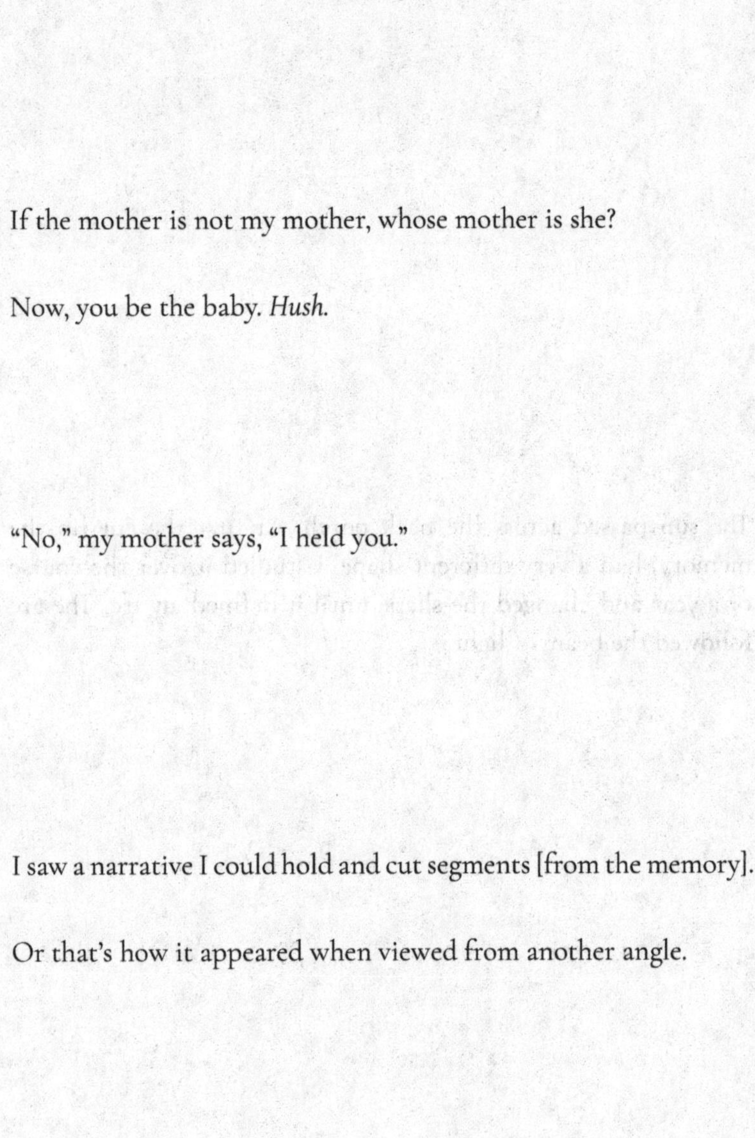

If the mother is not my mother, whose mother is she?

Now, you be the baby. *Hush.*

"No," my mother says, "I held you."

I saw a narrative I could hold and cut segments [from the memory].

Or that's how it appeared when viewed from another angle.

But when Charlie yelled, Mom's dog hid behind a chair, scratched the wall until her paws bled.

You know the expression, "Don't air your soiled laundry."

Carbon is the lifeblood of soil and the second most abundant element in the human body after oxygen. It first formed the interior of stars.

Since the arc is a slit across the sun's declination, the sun's angle over the course of a year, the noonday light would hit the opening one left for another.

In the emptied basement, my sister and I took turns pretending to be him, deepening our voices, strutting around. The way he expressed desire. "If you don't come to dinner, I'll kill you." And, jealous of Hildy, "Why don't you go fuck your dog!" Beneath our laughter was a sadness for Mom, maybe even for him: a deep muddy ditch with stagnant water we didn't want to smell. What we'd lost and would go on losing.

I stopped hearing the dog's bark, the key in the lock, Mom calling, "Time to set the table," the door slam, the smoke alarm sounding in the night. Mom drove me to an otolaryngologist. Hearing a beep in that brightly lit room, another in a far-off field, others in a mountain pass slick with ice, I raised my hand. "Above normal hearing," the doctor said. My mother's eyebrows raised. There was the tick of the office clock, the shuffle of the doctor's feet. No one asked what the child can't hear at home. The names he called my mother.

After writing this morning, I drive past the Pentecostal temple. The marquee reads:

> GOSSIP IS THE
> DEVIL'S RADIO ARE
> YOU HIS DJ!

When I was a child, I lived with a herd of wild horses. At times we stood beside cool streams, facing away from the wind so we could see what was coming that the wind did not carry.

When we galloped, I gripped the horse's mane. Later, I did not need to hold on. There was no separation between horse and child.

Amnesia of the moment. Amnesia of the decade. Forgot what he had done. The reds and oranges that rippled through her body didn't stop there. My body felt it, too. "Wake up," I pleaded.

As when I spooked the horse and my mother landed in the high grass in a heap. My hands on her cloud-white cheeks. "Wake up. *Please.*" When her eyes opened I said, "Tell me where you are." She didn't know. So I said, "The far field." I said, "Promise you'll remember." When her eyes opened again, she had no idea.

It happened over and over. For what seemed like a long, geologic time.

NO MONSTER, NO HERO

In a darkened room, my art professor projected slides of a house halved with a power saw so a slit of light shone through. It reminded me of something. I didn't know what. A split. A gap. A gasp. "Is it construction or deconstruction?" she asked. Reading new openings against old surfaces.

An abandoned space, tended.

Mom told me about the "Is Your Partner Abusive?" quizzes she took online. Clicking ovals as she remembered times when. "Does he isolate you from family?" "Does he withhold attention from you when he doesn't get his way?" "Does he not seem to notice or care how you feel?"

A: It happened all the time.

B: It didn't happen at all.

C. It neither happened nor didn't happen.

D. All of the above.

On the radio, a breaking story: one tower down, another on fire, daylight totally dark.

Days coded in red and orange.

The next week, Charlie brought Mom on a business trip to Manhattan. I took the train from college to join them for dinner. Ash still in the air, armed guards on corners. In the near-empty street, his voice blared at her.

Time blurred into no-time. My voice in capital letters, "NEVER TALK TO MY MOTHER THAT WAY."

When I felt afraid, I thought it meant I should call somebody else monster.

No monster, no hero.

"You're not her protector now, I am!" he shouted.

I gripped Mom's hand and led her away.

The horses and I traveled over twenty miles a day in search of greener pastures, like a memoir I once believed.

Firefighters, grief-faced after clearing debris, made a space for us at the bar. Mom pulled out her phone, "I need to tell him where we are." While we waited for his reply, I picked ash from her hair. *He needs taken care of,* I heard her say without saying.

In the margin of an earlier draft of this book, Mom wrote: "He really yelled at you."

I have no memory of that.

For the artist, my professor tells us, the hardest part of the project was getting to know the house. It seemed to take cutting through it with a chain saw, a heavy slow process performed on the surface.

On a stool by my dorm window, I peeled the white and purplish skins from garlic bulbs. Among garlic's sacred qualities: the ability to ward off malevolent spirits. I was making a new wedding dress for Mother. Fingers sticky with pulp, I stitched the garlic skins but only got as far as a sleeve.

When I called home, my sister explained, "I'm not keeping what he does to Mom from you. I'm keeping it from the role you play rescuing Mom."

When he spoke *at* my mother instead of *with* my mother, his heart contracted against reality.

Viewed from the distance of the moon, each of us is to Earth what atoms are to our bodies. There is no other. When the globe spun slowly, the continents, on their crustal plates, appeared separate.

When I spoke at him instead of with him—

Bacteria I swabbed from my belly button in class teemed under the microscope's eye. I pressed my own eye closer: the bacteria's constellations appeared separate from me. Dirty. If I conceived myself as separate, if I didn't share my pain, no one could touch me.

MOM: I didn't know you were suffering. You held it in.

At home, the first floor no longer had interior walls: vertical beams, salvaged from a collapsed barn, demarcated the rooms. Bit by bit, Mom found the bones of the house until there was nothing left to find.

"That is the antithesis of what actually happened," Mom says as she reads the book I have written about wild horses in search of nutrient-rich soil who, to protect themselves, communicate with a turn of the head, a flick of the ear. On which page she said it matters, and not remembering where, I've placed it here.

A family can see the same incident and believe it a shadow from a fallen tree, a curtain lifted by the breeze.

In another abandoned space: a majestic cut, a hole, an aperture, an oculus, an "eye" through which light shifts.

The [home] was no longer a fixed entity but a mutable space. Even the wall beneath the stairwell she cut away, revealing the red brick of the exterior. A bit of light shone through, which had been invisibly at play between the walls.

Her little things arranged on a dresser—in a single stroke he wiped them into the air.

"Don't make me do it," he said.

MOM: He could only hold it in for so long. Exploding at the dog or whatever, it came out.

Another time as he raged, Mom and I pressed our bodies to the bathroom door to keep him out. Part of me liked the feeling of pressing my body there, calling him monster.

From the hallway, sister whispered, "What are you doing?" I pulled her into the cramped room.

Why was I hiding in the bathroom? Why wasn't I in the backyard gazing at the stars?

When I believe *I* ends somewhere, and beyond it there are others, there goes the spacious quality of the mind.

There go the stars.

Inside the monster costume, Charlie was a little boy wiping tears from his cheeks without a sound. A roar at the cellular level shook the windowpanes.

I'd only heard about that boy secondhand. His stories were not for me to tell.

The feelings [I] buried, the self [I] abandoned, made a puppet of [me].

What if, when he threatened her, I had seen him as a scared horse, not a monster?

In the barn one night I watched two women tend a wound on a young stallion's leg. One of them touched the gash, and the horse reared, his hooves cutting a shaft of light. When he landed, eyes wide, ears flat, the crossties that held him snapped. It happened fast: the women wrestled the horse to the ground. They lay their bodies on top of the horse's body. The horse thrashed for a while, and then his breathing calmed. Something inside me shifted. They had not frozen or fled. They entered the space where the horse's body had risen into the air.

What if I entered the space where his temper rose into the air?

AN INKY SMUDGE

"Remember that time?" I'd say to Mom. "Remember that?" As if she needed me to make the world appear.

Did he really say that?

No, not him smiling in his apron. A neighbor said. Someone from the office said. Mom said. My sister and I said. The brain said. Despite what it heard.

After he stopped yelling and her dog stopped scratching to escape the house, Mom would scrub paw prints from the wall, the floor, the stairs.

MOM: I told myself, *This person has a temper and then calms down.*

In order to survive, the brain normalizes it, then atrophies.

My emotions? I put them out, like a dog in the rain. *You cannot come in*, I told them when they pawed the door. *You stink. There's no room for you here.*

What about my father? He was studying to administer general anesthesia for dental patients with high levels of anxiety. Local anesthesia lasts one and a half to two hours.

Anesthesia for the moment. Anesthesia for the pain.

The anesthesiologist's line: *Don't worry, you won't remember this when you wake up*, is precisely what worried me. I didn't remember. What else had I missed?

"Were you really where you said you'd be?" Charlie said and pushed her to the bed. Clouds gathered outside the window.

"This is not the life I imagined," Mom tells me.

Had I watched the surface of the lake while the horses grazed, I would have seen that the great drifts of cloud come and go, that I needn't identify with them, like the stories I told myself about our life.

MOM: What hurts most is the way he treated you.

Whatever I touched, whomever I loved, he didn't like.

It appeared it was me he was rallying against, but of course it was a part of himself.

MOM: Toward the end, it was one of the nonnegotiables of our marriage. I told him, "You may not talk about Emily, you may not say her name."

And here I’ve written a book in which my narrative of him appears.

I wrote "in which he appears" but crossed it out.

"You have to leave," I begged Mom.

She turned away.

Or, she turned toward the ceiling she was painting, a light she was hanging, floral drapes she was ironing for the front window.

Toward the dove with a hurt wing in a box she lined with the softest fabric.

MOM: I couldn't see a way out.

"I let him name me. I let his words define me. I wasn't calling myself. I was caught in his image of me, and that's why I believed him, and that's why I couldn't see clearly, and that's why I stayed."

The softest sound corresponds to air vibration as small as one tenth the diameter of an atom, which most infants can hear at birth. When the ear canal is smaller, the sound pressure generated is greater; loud sounds are even louder. One can also "hear" words inside one's head.

The names he called my mother.

Casting him as a monster I could say, *He is what I am not.*

Like deepfake tools that let users manipulate visual and audio content, animating old photos of relatives, etcetera. An eraser, white-out, the delete key, a line break replies: *He is what I am / not.*

The performance of a neural network is measured by its ability to reconstruct the original image from its representation in latent space.

As in: His head appears too large and more pixelated than his body.

I had forgotten how to let my mind be still like water. Forgotten the coming and going of an object doesn't alter water's ability to reflect. What did I need in order for the world to appear?

My phone lit up.

MOM: I'm at the grocery store. Quiet. I saw him texting another woman last night. Thought I was sleeping. Does not know I know.

Oh, Mom.

MOM: I keep wondering if I'm doing the right thing to leave him. Because he has remained very nice. So this is just what I needed to get back on track.

Mom handed me a scrap of paper with a name. Deep circles under her eyes. "It's the woman he's been texting," she said. "If I search her name, he might trace it in my history."

On my phone, many faces appeared.

"That's her!" I shouted, "That's her!" separating the parts at the point of collapse. I pinched and spread my fingers on the screen, zooming in on the image. Not-building, not-to-rebuild, not-built-space.

"If I leave him," she said later that week.

"If?" I asked.

"It isn't easy to walk away from someone you love."

“Summer—,” she said to my sister and me, “This summer I’ll leave him.

“That’s different from what you said yesterday.”

I approached a wall of photographs at his mother's house and saw, to my horror, someone had made Mom's face an inky smudge, a few curls of her hair left sticking out.

Whose face have I made an inky smudge?

For a long time, nobody said, *That never happened*, because in the first place nobody said, *That happened.*

"I was taking a shower, and he came at me, and his hands came through the water and grabbed my neck."

MOM: Don't tell the neck part. It's not even accurate. He didn't put his hands around my neck in the shower. He'd stand at the door and say terrible things to me and watch me in tears.

In the kitchen one night, he pulled his fist back and said, "I'm going to kill you."

"Remember that?" I said to Mom.

A FLOOD OF SUNSHINE

In an old growth forest at night, mom photographs the trees. We want the photographs she takes to reveal what we can't see with our own eyes—the orbs we've heard are here.

But here in the dark, among the trees, I see the orbs.

Aloft, floating, exuberant things, in varying colors and sizes. Over and over I point.

"Where?" Mom spins around. Although she can't see them, she snaps photos of the air.

When I pointed, Mom never said, *There's nothing to see.*

Mom said, "Where? Where?" Believing.

Later, in the hotel room, we sat on the edge of her bed. On the camera screen: around the trunks of trees, dark night and spheres of light like stars, some small enough to fit in a hand. The orbs I'd seen in the forest. "Look at this one!" Mom exclaimed again and again, magnifying the image. Although I loved her excitement, I grew tired. What could she see that I was missing, her eyes welling with tears?

And she left him.

I saw the story I was telling myself: White light, deep blue. It wasn't the invisible made visible. But the visible made invisible made visible again.

NOTES

Preface

"Matta-Clark's site-specific, abstract geometric cut-aways evoke (and subvert) much 20th century art historical discourse [...] This is most obvious in the majestic cut he made at New York City's Pier 52 in 1975, called 'Days End' [...]." "40 Years After His Death Gordon Matta Clark Takes on New Relevance" from *Hyperallergic*, Joseph Nechvatal, September 4, 2018.

"If a grain of salt would like to measure the degree of saltiness of the ocean, to have a perception of the saltiness of the ocean, it drops itself into the ocean and becomes one with it, and the perception is perfect [...] When [nuclear physicists] get deeply into the world of subatomic particles, they see their mind in it. An electron is first of all your concept of the electron. The object of your study is no longer separated from your mind." Thich Nhất Hạnh, *Being Peace*, 1987.

Proof

"The act of cutting through from one space to another produces a certain complexity involving depth perception. Aspects of stratification probably interest me more than the unexpected views which are generated by the removals—not the surface, but the thin edge, the severed surface that reveals the autobiographical process of its making. There is a kind of complexity which comes from taking an otherwise completely normal, conventional, albeit anonymous situation and redefining it, retranslating it into overlapping and multiple readings of conditions past and present. Each building generates its own unique situation." "Gordon Mata-Clarke's Building Dissections," an interview by Donald Wall from

Arts Magazine, May 1976. Rpt. *Gordon Matta-Clarke*, ed. Corine Diserens.

"Viewed from the distance of the moon, the astonishing thing about the earth, catching the breath, is that it is alive. The photographs show the dry, pounded surface of the moon in the foreground, dead as an old bone. Aloft, floating free beneath the moist, gleaming membrane of bright blue sky, is the rising earth, the only exuberant thing in this part of the cosmos. If you could look long enough, you would see the swirling of the great drifts of white cloud, covering and uncovering the half-hidden masses of land. If you had been looking a very long, geologic time, you could have seen the continents themselves in motion, drifting apart on their crustal plates, held aloft by the fire beneath. It has the organized, self-contained look of a live creature, full of information, marvelously skilled in handling the sun." Lewis Thomas, *The Lives of a Cell*, 1978.

Enough

Wallace Stevens, *The Auroras of Autumn*, 1950.

Eating Trash

"I was always looking for some way to incorporate the whole space. And since it was a tremendous void with very little surface in it, except for the outside surface and the pier, I kept on thinking of ways to correlate parts. That is, how to make an opening in one section work with other openings. It was really a matter of trying different intersects together." "Gordon Matta-Clarke: Dilemmas," a radio interview by Liza Bear, WBAI-FM, New York, March 1976. Rpt. *Gordon Matta-Clarke*, ed. Corine Diserens.

"Well, in every case, yeah [my] intrusion has to do with [an existing] structural interpretation. And so originally the idea came from watching the sun as it passed across the floor. Of course it defined an arc. And so the segments of arc which were cut at first in the roof, directly above the canal or moat in the center, was a shape that was generated by a series of points—three centers, basically—three arcs intersecting and forming that shape, what we call a spherical section, in a stylization of a spherical surface. And which came, of course, from associations and references to the sun and earth surface relationship." Ibid.

"My earliest contacts with other people were not in the street, but from one window sill to another, in that typical Italian way of hanging out your window. [...] Sill pals. That's the way I made contact with a lot of people. There was even an older couple who remained friends of the family for years—they became friends because we—my twin brother and I—were always hanging out the windows and they were afraid. It's interesting, the space I remember most is not so much floors and shelter as openings into other spaces and other people's realms... A window-punctured world, right?" "Gordon Matta-Clarke: Splitting the Humphrey Street Building," an interview by Liza Bear from *Avalanche*, December 1974. Rpt. in *Gordon Matta-Clarke*, ed. Corine Diserens.

And when you have divided all the bones,
And searched right down amid the very marrow,
You should look and ask the question:
Where is "thingness" to be found?

Shantideva in Pema Chödrön's *No Time to Lose: A Timely Guide to the Way of the Bodhisattva*, 5.63, 2005.

"After I made the ceiling cut, I studied it. At first it had a very different shape—I changed the shape over the [course] of two weeks—[to see] how it went across the floor. And I wanted to make that opening work over the span of a year so that it was, in fact, related to a floor cut. So the floor cut then was going to be an arc that would follow the progress of that beam of light across the floor, over a period of months. But the only way to do that was by making a slit. So the slit is in fact a zenith point, the zenith intersect of the floor and roof hole. And of course since it's a slit across the sun's [declination], the sun's angle over the course of a year, the noonday or zenith light will hit that opening and it will hit the water from one end of the year to the next, so it's very precise. Also it cuts the space I designated for the piece—the open space of the pier—in half. So it's the center." "Gordon Matta-Clarke: Dilemmas," a radio interview by Liza Bear, WBAI-FM, New York, March 1976. Rpt. *Gordon Matta-Clarke*, ed. Corine Diserens.

No Monster, No Hero

"The hardest part of the whole project was getting to know the building. It seemed to take cutting through it with a chain saw to get to know it. Once that heavy slow process was performed on the surfaces, then the other ideas were simple." "Gordon Matta-Clarke: Splitting the Humphrey Street Building," an interview by Liza Bear from *Avalanche*, December 1974. Rpt. in *Gordon Matta-Clarke*, ed. Corine Diserens.

"I beveled [the foundation] at an angle dictated by one course of cinder block. First we scored and chiseled away all the block reinforcing the foundation as we worked, until the rear half of the house was standing on four points at the corners. Then, using building jacks, we transferred the load, about fifteen tons of it, from the final blocks, and just lowered it. Throughout this whole process, there was a terrific suspense, not really knowing what would hold or shift, but the structure acted perfectly, responding to the jacks and lowering process without a groan. She came down like a dream... The whole event gave me new insight into what a house is, how solidly built, how easily moved. It was like a perfect dance partner. [...] [W]hat I mean is that the realization of motion in a static structure was exhilarating." Ibid.

"*A W-Hole House* was the beginning of an idea which was developed over a year with *Splitting* and *Bingo X Ninths* [*Bingo*]. These projects took most of their energy from the object-like treatment of the suburban home. Buildings are fixed entities in the minds of most people. The notion of mutable space is taboo especially in one's own house. People live in their space with a temerity that is frightening. Home owners generally do little more than maintain their property. Once an institution like the home is objectified in such a way, it does understandably raise a moral issue. These issues are not ones that I'm involved in but continue to inspire criticism from defenders of home and property." "Interview with Gordon Matta-Clarke, Antwerp, September, 1977" from the catalogue *Gordon Matta-Clarke, Internationaal Cultureel Centrum*, Antwerp, 1977. Rpt, in *Gordon Matta-Clarke*, ed. Corine Diserens.

"What is invisibly at play behind a wall of floor, once exposed, becomes an active participant in a spatial drawing of the building's inner life." Ibid.

An Inky Smudge

"Completion through removal. Abstractions of surfaces. Not-building, not-to-rebuild, not-built-space. Creating spatial complexity, reading new openings against old surfaces. Light admitted into space or beyond surfaces that are cut. Breaking and entering. Approaching structural collapse, separating the parts at the point of collapse." Gordon Matta-Clark, *Manifesto*, 1971.

A Flood of Sunshine

"A Flood of Sunshine" is named from after a chapter title in Nathaniel Hawthorne's *The Scarlet Letter*, 1850.

ACKNOWLEDGMENTS

Excerpts appeared in the following journals: *Another Chicago Magazine*, *Speculative Nonfiction*, *swamp pink*, and *Prism Review*, where "Wild Horses" shared the 2025 Staff Choice Award. Thanks to all involved. Immense thanks to Eric Muhr and the team at Fernwood Press.

Gratitude to my mom whose wisdom and ability to create beauty and magic, particularly in the face of difficulty, uplifts and guides me and so many others. To my dad and Cyndi for your unconditional love and generosity. To John for joy and music and lunchbox notes. To my sisters Callie and Annie and Taylor for your friendship; I am so grateful we are together in this life.

Gratitude to Robin Clarke, Thomas Page McBee, and Meg Shevenock for your friendship, insight, astute edits, and helping me to see a way through. To Josh Zelesnick, Rachel Nelson, Joy Katz, Toi Derricotte, Rachel Zucker, Charlie Legere, Faith Barrett, and Sarah Marxer. To Borland Garden, Art in the Garden, Olmo Ling, Zero Prestige, Real People, and the poetmom listserve. To my teachers and my students. To Gail Hunter, Iris Grossman, and Tempa Dukte Lama. I do not know how to say the thanks I feel.

Finally, deep bows of gratitude to Sten for all you have loved into life with your gentle, steady presence and for being with me on this journey. And to our children for shining your light in this world, for your questions and songs and chants and visions and all of who you are.

www.ingramcontent.com/pod-product-compliance
Lightning Source LLC
LaVergne TN
LVHW030922080826
845145LV00013B/3021

* 9 7 8 1 5 9 4 9 8 2 2 8 6 *